Life on the

Texas Range

Number Fourteen   The M. K. Brown Range Life Series

The prints reproduced in this book were made in 1936 by Erwin E. Smith for the Texas Centennial celebration. In the 1952 edition they were reproduced by sheet-fed gravure; the present edition is printed in 300-line offset. The prints are part of a permanent display of Smith's range photography in

THE TEXAS MEMORIAL MUSEUM

ERWIN E. SMITH

Life on the
Texas Range

Photographs by

ERWIN E. SMITH

Text by

J. EVETTS HALEY

University of Texas Press. Austin

International Standard Book Number 0-292-74605-9
Library of Congress Catalog Card Number 52-13181
Copyright © 1952 by the University of Texas Press
All rights reserved
Printed in the United States of America
Fourth Printing, 1984

Requests for permission to reproduce material from
this work should be sent to Permissions, University
of Texas Press, Box 7819, Austin, Texas 78712.

List of Plates

[1] This print was made by Erwin E. Smith from an old photographic plate in his possession.

Life on the
Texas Range

Erwin E. Smith

A Biographical Introduction

Erwin E. Smith

ERWIN E. SMITH was the outstanding cowboy photographer of the West. At the beginning of the century in Texas he was doing on sensitized plates and film what Charles Russell was doing in paint for Montana, and what Emerson Hough was trying to do in print for the cowmen of the West. He was recording them true to life.

As a boy quietly burning with ambition to ride the range, he conceived the idea of such a record of the cowboys of Texas. With precocious insight he realized that their work was the vital, vivid thing that set these light-reined riders in a world apart. He saw that this work was an art in itself. He saw too, with the regret that seizes all lovers of the undulating seas of grass, that the steady inroads of the plow seemed to be pushing these booted and broad-crowned men — men sitting lightly in their saddles as they swept at a long lope across the ranges of Texas — into the pages of the past.

Erwin Smith headed west with his riggin' and a simple camera and set to work. His youthful affection for the ways of the West deepened into his first, and seasoned into his last, love. His sense of telling and accurate detail, his unstaged but imaginative compositions, and his rugged insistence on honest action and incident, with his "colossal patience" over years of financially unremunerative work, were nothing short of the nature and the devotion of the real artist.

The result was a voluminous collection of prints that illustrated the life of the range better than anything else in existence. This accomplishment alone would have assured him a place in history among men who dearly love horses and somehow always hope to profit on cattle. But the story of Erwin Smith is more than that.

He was bred to the frontier. His maternal great-grandfather, Samuel Erwin, a native of Virginia, pushed into pioneer Tennessee, where he was married to Sallie Rogers Crisp by an individualistic justice of the peace by the name of David Crockett. Samuel Erwin made several moves with his growing family before joining the eager trend to Texas in 1837 and settling just south of Red River, in Lamar County. Two years later he moved to

15

the Blue Prairie, in Fannin County, and in 1842 settled among a motte of trees, teeming with bees, at a spot that became known as Honey Grove. Here his youngest son, Samuel Augustus, married Elizabeth Drennon and became a stock farmer.[1]

The Smith family came in from the South, and in time Albert Alexander Smith met and married Nancy, a daughter of Samuel Augustus Erwin. Smith went into the mercantile business at Honey Grove, and there, about ninety miles northeast of Dallas and just south of Red River, his only son, Erwin Evans Smith, was born, August 22, 1886.

Erwin's father was a quiet, gallant Southern gentleman with a good business head and a passion for orderly work and living. As a consequence his business prospered and he became well established in the little town. Erwin's mother, a sensitive person, had, as a young lady, been sent from the upper Texas frontier for education at St. Mary's, an Episcopal boarding school at Raleigh, North Carolina. She painted with ability and was more interested in artistic pursuits than in housekeeping or in business. In her comfortable home she indulged her bent while becoming, in her son's own words, "a genuine lover of the country and all nature."

Except for the quiet gentility of his father, Erwin Smith was his mother's son. The commercial world brashly pushed itself upon him. And while of necessity he battled with its problems, nothing but his ardent love of the cow country ever seemed to concern him unduly. Business and clocks and schedules were not for him. As with Andy Adams' old cowman, there was always "ample time." Economic success and routine living were for those stolid, unimaginative souls who never ventured, either actually or vicariously, upon the hurricane deck of a cow horse across the quivering waves of wind-blown grass.

Yet this lack of a sense of the business side of living was Erwin Smith's galloping nemesis. It was the misunderstood and wholly unruly mount in his life's remuda of interests and problems. Were it not futile, or perhaps presumptuous, to question the ways of nature, this might be said to have been the tragic shortcoming that blighted his career. At least it stopped him far short of the ambitious career that as a boy he had imaginatively mapped and promisingly launched to turn to account the unusual artistic abilities that reached far beyond his skill with shutter and lens. Instead he was fated to struggle with debt for years while quietly, and even pathetically, cherishing his one true love — perpetuation in artistic form of the life of the ranges of Texas.

Erwin was about four years old when his father died of pneumonia, leaving his family with a fairly comfortable estate by the standards of the time and place. Eventually Mrs. Smith was remarried, to Percy H. White of Bonham, who was likewise of Southern antecedents, and also a merchant. He too was a practical person, sternly convinced that the first duty of a man is to make some money, the wherewithal to a decent living, which, to a few, still seems a reasonable point of view. But in nature's wise way it is given to youth to dream.

[1] *Biographical Souvenir of the State of Texas* (Chicago, 1889), 282–83.

Beyond the streams and woodlands, far beyond the shaded vistas of Erwin's home, was an open world scornful of turning plows and routine living, a world of dry air and shimmering light that shriveled the skins but freed the souls of venturesome men who loved and lived with horses. Not the humdrum affairs of a cooped-up general store, but the infinite plains of Texas, were the world for Erwin Smith. An affection that almost became an affliction took hold of him when as a child of eight he visited the JCS Ranch in Foard County, Texas. There on the ranch owned by his uncle, John Sanders, he rode and learned something of the intricacies of proper work with cattle.

From then on, Erwin's lengthening, lanky body seemed to take its somnolent ease wherever abstract time found him, while in detached nature his mind, heart, and soul ranged wide with the cowboys. Yet daily through the allotted terms, he made his dreaming way to the Bonham schools in that routine that is still generally accepted as a substitute for education, while the family, with business affairs safely under control by Mr. White, lived well in a large frame house distinguished by huge columns suggestive of Southern Colonial style.

Among Erwin's closest boyhood friends was Harry Peyton Steger. Steger, who gained youthful fame in the literary world, recalled that when the two met at Bonham, Erwin "wore the nine-year-old boy's terrific adaptation of what his vivid imagination tells him cowboys wear."

These two gifted youngsters grew up in Bonham together, in a country that was, as Steger said, "well out of the geography of cowboys, but well within the circle of true Western atmosphere." On Saturdays the Bonham square was crowded with covered wagons from the country. The heavy air buzzed with soft Texas voices, and tinkled as with tiny bells as many teams stood in their chain harness and persistently switched at flies. There were no cars, but boys then had horses.

Steger told of the times when he and Erwin, "constantly in a state of insulting challenge against those other presuming young gentlemen who owned steeds thought to be wind-speedy," rode through Bonham with abandon. It was then a joyous thing for recklessly riding men of twelve, imaginary six-shooters on their hips and the dangerous trail before them, to jog through the throng and then whip the air into a stiff breeze, full in their faces, as they raced for the open country, Harry Peyton on Lady Gray, pitted against Erwin proudly mounted on Sir Black.[2]

Throughout his youth Erwin made other trips to the JCS outfit and took part in stray work on the larger ranches in the same region. He early acquired a box camera and diligently set to work recording the life of the range, while learning to develop his films and make the prints at home. At sixteen he came near dying of typhoid. The completeness of his obsession with the West by then may be judged from the fact that his long delirium

[2] Harry Peyton Steger, "A Texas Boy in Boston and His Work in Western Art," *Holland's Magazine*, June, 1909, p. 26.

was frequently and violently accentuated by his jumping up in bed and appearing to cut loose with a six-shooter at an imaginary Indian. Again he would jump on a mythical horse and go loping off across the range. But at last he was better and, during his slow recovery, again at work with camera and film. In his quiet, sensitive, and unobtrusive way, he had, in introspective maturity, definitely settled on his purpose in life. In this he had the whole-hearted support of his artistic mother, and the financial backing, somewhat skeptically tendered, of his practical step-father.

Erwin returned to the cow country with his camera slung over his saddle horn and went to work as a regular hand. From the JCS and association with his seasoned cowboy uncle and cousin, he rode off to other, larger outfits throughout "the breaks," the unplowed broken country between the Cross Timbers and the High Plains. He followed the roundups with the Three Circles, V-Pigpens, OX's and R2's, working with the wagon, taking pictures, almost always in deep and detached thought with his own plans.

When he was about eighteen he left the cow country for Chicago to seek association with Lorado Taft, one of the outstanding sculptors of his time. He had made up his mind to learn to model and put in bronze the life of the ranges of Texas. He found Taft a great and admirable teacher. "Each pupil was to him the only one," Smith recalled. "I was with him two years, and got all my formal training from him. But it was formal, only, and I felt like I wanted to work on the subjects I knew best." He decided that study in Boston was the next step in his training. Yet a question persisted in his mind: Did he know the life of the range, that fascinating study course from which no man ever graduates—did he know his subject well enough? At the same time, his decision to try Boston bumped into the disconcerting realization that the great ranges of Texas were being broken up, and that their ways were radically changing.

"I knew that the life wouldn't wait," he said simply, "and that the technique would. So I put off Boston as long as I could." He returned to the cow outfits of Texas with a camera "so modest that the results" which he achieved with it were "all the more surprising. He carried an Eastman screen-focus Kodak, with Goerz lens and volute shutter," his only equipment besides "a strong liking for photography and an appreciation of its possibilities." His work became noted for its absolute fidelity and, as one writer claimed, for settings "unrivalled in America in contrasts." His pictures were models of composition, like well-done paintings, and like paintings captured that indefinable quality that is known as atmosphere. They seemed to "breathe the spirit of the cattle country." [3]

Smith spent much of his time on the larger outfits because their work with cattle closely approximated that of the open range. Like most cowpunchers, he never said much about his itinerary, if he had one. With saddle, bedroll, riggin', and camera, he followed

[3] George Pattullo, "Glimpses of Cowboy Life in Texas," *Photo-Era,* June, 1908, p. 201; Harry Peyton Steger, "Photographing the Cowboy as He Disappears," *World's Work,* January, 1909, p. 11111; and Catherine Wharton's fine series in the *Sherman* (Texas) *Democrat,* September 27 to October 2, 1934.

"the work," the general roundups. He drifted up Red River to the old Shoe Bars and took a raft of pictures on the pioneer JA outfit, a ranch that still measures its acres by generous lines along the colorful canyons of the Palo Duro. In the summer of 1907 he was hard at work on the undulating grasslands along the Canadian in the western Panhandle.

Some of his outstanding pictures of men, horses, and cattle, both in dramatic action and in peaceful repose, were made on the LS Ranch, west of Amarillo, on land still redolent of the zestful days of the open range. These include the much-used scenes at Old Tascosa, the first range town in the western Panhandle, where frontier life is long since gone, but where thirst persistently and understandably lingers.[4]

While he was never reluctant to catch the cowboy at his diversions, Erwin Smith was primarily interested in him as a working hand. "The real cowboy," as he emphasized to his friend Steger, "is essentially a worker." Contrary to the popular impression, Smith pointed out, "he doesn't overdress, for he cannot and do his work. . . . His hours are long and exact much of him."

Again he pointed out that the old-time puncher lived a hard life. "At times it is nothing but hardship; yet there are so many features of it that appeal . . . that once a man has done a certain amount of it, he isn't content with any other existence."

Combined with Smith's early ambition to portray the cowboy was his concern over the lurid but popular misrepresentation of the breed. In effect, he early became a sort of defensive cowboy historian. He fervently hoped to blow away, with the wind and dust of reality, the false aura built up around the range; to dispel the make-believe with the tangible, factual, and far more interesting elements of its rigorous life and action.[5] From the first he seemed to know just what he wanted to record: the life of the range itself, as simple, direct, and honest as hard labor can make it, and yet at times as colorful and dramatic as zestful living, danger, and death can provide. Smith was an appreciative part of it. Yet he viewed it keenly and objectively with a critical eye. He became a genuine student of the cattle range.

He found that no set pattern guided the cowboy at his daily work. This man rode in a world of constantly shifting action and changing problems — problems not only depending on the economics of an inviolable natural order but arising out of, and constantly changing with, the vagaries of climate and topography and the whims, the caprices, and the psychology of the animals he rode and handled.

Therefore as Smith worked from one large outfit to another, he learned the adapta-

---

[4] Tascosa, the second settlement in the Panhandle region, was started in 1877, enjoyed ten years of colorful life, and began its decline with the completion of the Fort Worth and Denver Railway and the founding of Amarillo in 1887. See J. Evetts Haley, *The XIT Ranch of Texas* (Chicago, 1929), 195–205, and *George W. Littlefield, Texan* (Norman, Oklahoma, 1943), 80–99, for something of its history.

[5] For his emphasis on the cowboy as a working hand, see Steger's "Photographing the Cowboy as He Disappears," *World's Work,* January, 1909, p. 11120; and George Pattullo, in the *Boston Herald,* January 12, 1908.

tions that varying terrain, climate, and vegetation force upon the cowboys who successfully cope with nature's problems. He learned the value of sure-footed mules in the roughest country, learned how to stake a horse on the treeless plains, how to pull bog along the Canadian, how to gather outlaw steers in the breaks of the Matadors, how to handle the sensitive point of a great herd without balling the drive up, and how to lighten the load of a swimming horse in a churning, boiling flood. Through many years with the best outfits he learned the skilled and artful ways of work that distinguish the light-riding genuine cowhand from the soggy-seated country boy draped like a bag of mush all over his horse and saddle.

All of which served him in good stead, not only in the pursuit of his work but in keeping him intact in life and limb. For the same sort of incident that befalls every rider of the wide seas of grass came his way. Once, on his return to the LS Ranch from Old Tascosa, on the north side of the Canadian, he was cut off by a sudden flood. The prospect was bad as he eased into the water. His good river mount took the wide and turgid current with the same eager expectancy that fine horses and fond men show as they turn their steps toward home. But shortly he began hitting the treacherous pockets cut by the swirling currents of the river in its unpredictable beds of quicksand. Twice man and mount went under. Then Erwin slid from the saddle and grabbed his drowning horse by the tail. With lightened load the floundering animal breasted the current and towed his rider to safety on the other side.

For several years through the busiest seasons Erwin followed the roundups. He lived with the chuck wagons. He studied the range bosses, the wagon cooks, the horse wranglers, and the cowboys in their daily work, recording all its significant features graphically and in great detail. An observer on the LS Ranch in 1907 marveled that "he seemed to be everywhere at once, taking pictures all the time." But the secret of his work went deeper than that. Among Smith's papers are many penciled sketches, worthy bits of art in themselves. They were preliminary compositions of men and cattle and horses in diverse settings and situations. They were the compositions he wished to catch as the men he lived with moved without let or hindrance at their skillful work. To achieve them he had to anticipate the weather, the light and shadow, the lay of the land, and the resultant movement of men and cattle. Now, roundups are made of economic necessity, not to provide a setting for any photographer. If one of these variable factors bearing upon Smith's projected composition went wrong, his entire plan was completely ruined. Compositions planned far in advance were often put off because the herd moved a different way, because a vagrant cloud moved across the sun, because the unstaged remuda trotted out of range, or because the uncooperative cows that composed the drags befogged the world with dust. Sometimes a picture that he had planned for weeks could not be made because of nature's variable factor until another roundup was held the following year. No wonder Steger called his patience "colossal."

There was well-laid plan in Smith's movements as recorded by the observer on the LS Ranch. He recalled that as the LS boss and hands threw the drive together, Smith "rode past at a dead run, raced to the top of a rocky hill, dismounted, dropped his bridle reins in true cowboy fashion, and was ready to photograph the herd as the boys pushed them across Parker Creek and corralled them in the branding pen." Thus Smith carefully figured perspective, setting, and action in recording a life where settings were always changing and action would never wait.

Many of Smith's best pictures were made with the LS outfit. Here he caught the day herder on a "ga'nt" horse, watching his cows from a high point on the rim of the cap rock above the valley of the Canadian. Here he showed the boss staking his night horse without a stake pin, simply by digging a little hole in the sod with his pocketknife and tamping the knotted end of his rope in it. Here he made the striking pictures of Zack Burkett, the boss, and Isabel Guerele, pioneer Mexican horse wrangler and friend of Billy the Kid, as they pulled a cow from under a boulder where she had slipped and fallen. And it was from the LS headquarters that they all rode into Old Tascosa, hell-bent to slake their thirst at Jack Cooper's bar.

Once in awhile the men of the range found diversion, in poker and mumble-peg, but mainly their diverse work was likewise their play. Real cowboys could then be rounded up in droves at twenty-five dollars per head per month. As may be suspected, it was not the pay but the zestful life alone that made life worth living, as well as worth recording. During this period Erwin Smith was riding happily and high.[6]

When the work was done that fall, Smith said good-bye to the cowboys on the LS and returned to Bonham to take the next carefully designed step in his career. He loaded his trunk with cowboy pictures and left for the East, again to study art. He cut quite a figure as he walked down the streets of Boston, his lanky six-foot frame topped off with a big hat from under which an obtruding shock of heavy black hair threatened to fall in confusion across the bridge of his prominent nose.

Undoubtedly he felt a little ill at ease, like most men of the soil in sophisticated sur-roundings, as those proper Bostonians improperly turned to stare. But what he lacked in momentary poise he made up in resolute determination as his short-clipped gait in cowboy boots—the walk of men uncomfortably out of place upon the ground—carried him directly to the Museum of Fine Arts. There he modestly and quietly enrolled with the art classes in sketching and sculpture.

With his years of observations on the cattle ranges of Texas, and an estimated two thousand pictures to work from, he was determined to learn to model and cast the cowboy in lasting bronze. He wanted to do his subject right, not as a "rootin', tootin', shootin'" swaggering son-of-a-gun, as popular imagination had him, but as a proud man on horseback

---

[6] For something of his work on the LS Ranch, see Dulcie Sullivan, "Cowboy Photographer," *The Cattleman*, June, 1951, pp. 101–102.

in hard, skillful, and dangerous, and hence intriguing, work. Erwin Smith had just turned twenty-one and he had a man's job to do.

Erwin settled himself at the Boston Museum of Fine Arts for three years' work with Bela Lyon Pratt, who encouraged his departure from the formal courses. "He said I was right," Smith recalled, "about doing what I was interested in, with the materials I had in hand." Some of Smith's early efforts were turned toward catching the strong facial characteristics of the American Indian. He modeled from memory the bust of American Horse, a Sioux Indian. It brought a prize and recognition when shown at the Boston Art Institute and placed on display at the Boston Art Club. But his studies of the Kiowa chieftain Lone Wolf and of a Nez Percé chief, done in Pratt's studio, were more to his own liking. His bust of old Ed Bomar, range boss of the Turkey Tracks, was perhaps his best work.

While Smith was busy on the Sioux model, Pratt was commissioned to design an Indian profile for what became known as the "buffalo nickel." Pratt, though a distinguished artist, knew little about Indians. When he mentioned the matter to Smith, his student "hauled out a round dozen of magnificent portrait pictures he had made of chiefs and braves of western tribes, and the two men studied them over. . . . They hit on the idea of a profile that would be a composite of them all: Fighting Bear, Black Thunder, Blue Horse, Iron Shell, Low Cedar, Yellow Elk and the rest." If anyone should have particular credit, according to Smith, it would be Yellow Elk, a Rosebud, South Dakota, Sioux. With Erwin's help the design was made.[7]

Thus Erwin's pictures attracted immediate attention, and he was asked to show a representative group at the opening of a Boston art center. The showing was made, and the news that here was something extraordinary got around.

At that time a brilliant young Canadian writer of positive Scotch breeding, physiognomy, and character, who was then serving as Sunday editor of the *Boston Herald,* was pondering the warning of his doctor that the fast pace of his work and life demanded a change of climate. When he heard of Smith's pictures, suggestive of something completely out of that world, George Pattullo went down to see for himself. With quick and imaginative insight, he saw more than the source materials for sculpture in Erwin Smith's pictures. He saw the wide sweep of the West, the vigor and the violence of its action, and the drama of men daily working with danger and gaily flirting with death. Considering his determined nature, Pattullo suddenly became amenable to his doctor's suggestions. The West looked like the proper place for him. For both artist and writer fate must have smiled to herself as she unobtrusively spun the wheel of human destiny.

[7] The impression persisted, for years, that James Earle Fraser designed "the whole of the buffalo nickel," and that a tourist attraction for the Northern Pacific Railroad at Glacier National Park, Chief Two Guns White Calf, was the model. The magazine *Time,* March 26, 1934, noting Two Guns' passing, contradicted his claim but gave credit to Fraser. Smith, with his passion for honest detail, was anxious to correct the inaccuracy: Fraser produced only the buffalo. See Catherine Wharton's series of articles on Smith in the *Sherman* (Texas) *Democrat,* October 1, 1934.

The immediate result was Pattullo's enthusiastic appraisal of Smith and his work in a full-page illustrated article in the Sunday *Herald*, January 12, 1908, in which he fully anticipated that the Texan punching clay cows around the Boston Museum of Fine Arts would eventually become a great artist. Thus the benign winds of taste and approval began to blow in Erwin's direction, and they stimulated him no less than the sandstorms of West Texas, though in an entirely different way.

Smith had already become known as something of an authority upon the range. Dustin Farnum, an old favorite of the silent western films starring in "The Ranger," had seen his pictures and sought his advice to avoid inaccuracies in the portrayal of the West. Smith was anxious to help, for the painting of the cow country in false colors had already become a burden to him.

He thought Frederic Remington "a paragon of accuracy" compared to most artists, though he found serious fault with Remington's "Broncho Buster," a bronze cast especially as a gift from the Rough Riders to Theodore Roosevelt. But the measure of his sound technical knowledge and seasoned judgment at twenty-one was his confident assertion that Charles Russell was the only artist whose work "faithfully portrays the cowboy life and conveys the spirit of the country." And the reason as Smith expressed it was an unconscious commentary on the virtues of his own work. Russell, he said, "has the exact knowledge necessary to the work. He has caught the atmosphere of the great cattle country—indeed, he is a part of it."

Pattullo elaborated to say that Erwin's marvelous sense of composition showed in every picture, even as his artistic nature showed in his sensitive face and hands. But more than composition and action were revealed in these unusual prints, Pattullo continued. "It is because he knows the life so thoroughly; it is because he has caught and felt the nameless indefinable spirit of the vast cattle country that he feels it and the men and things that go to make it up."[8] Smith himself was in his pictures.

From this initial meeting grew a long and intimate association between the easygoing Texan and the vigorous Canadian whose warring line ran back through the Scottish Highlands for many centuries. The brash young Pattullo, quite sensitive now to the suggestions of his doctor, likewise felt that Boston could wait, and that even the Sunday *Herald* could struggle along without him. The Texas range was just the place for him and Erwin Smith.

The summer of 1908 found them among the cowboys. They made their way to the JA Ranch, near Clarendon, where Pattullo, with quick and ready wit, seemed to convince the outfit that no comparable influence had hit the Palo Duro since its dominant Goodnight quit wearing a gun. The boys wangled horses from the wagon boss, threw their bedrolls into the chuck wagon, and watched it rumble off toward camp on Dinner Creek.

Smith was again in his element, while the sharp and observant Pattullo, soaking up

[8] George Pattullo, "From Bronco Buster to Boston Art Student," *Boston Herald*, January 12, 1908.

every detail, soon had the material for a horse story called "Blackie," the first that he sold to the *Saturday Evening Post*. Among Smith's better pictures taken here was that of the outfit eating breakfast at four in the morning. Since he had no modern flashgun, he simply set his camera and flashed the picture by having Pattullo throw some gunpowder into the cook's fire.

In time the boys decided to drift across the Quitaque country and get a taste of cowboy life on the bitter waters of Croton Breaks. They found the Matadors much to their liking. This outfit, too, was run in the old-time tradition, and it was here that Smith got some of his best cutting-horse pictures—the hardest of all to catch in the open—and his series on the technique of handling outlaw cattle. It was here that he caught George Pattullo and Harry Campbell, son of the founder of the ranch, in front of a dugout rigging up for the fall hunt. From the Matadors, Pattullo and Smith set out for central New Mexico, and spent some time on the Bar W, near Carrizozo. Then with their saddles and bedrolls packed in a buckboard, they skirted the mountains and headed toward the rough, hard-riding Blocks, to the west of Roswell. On the way they fell in with an old nester named Ed Banty, with his wife and a bevy of kids in a covered wagon, and a bunch of mongrel dogs that trotted faithfully in its moving shade, their long tongues lolling. The party camped at a lake along the way, where Erwin got the wonderfully atmospheric picture at dusk—"The Nester at the Water Hole."

Around the fire that night, Banty, who turned out to be a reverent old fellow, insisted on prayer for all in camp. As the cool evening fell and the celestial altar lights glowed, Banty heatedly argued religion with the eager, positive young Pattullo. Despairing of making much impression on the square-jawed Scot, he got the two young adventurers down on the sod in divine supplication. "O Lord," he pleaded in concern over Pattullo's apostasy, "pluck this brand from the burning."

While Erwin considered the figure in the light of photography, Pattullo was spiritually unmoved. Contentious youth stubbornly holds to its convictions, and Banty finally decided that Pattullo's soul was lost, since he contended that the earth was round. If he really thought so, Banty insisted, how could he explain the Revelation of St. John the Divine of "four angels standing on the four corners of the earth"? Pattullo could not explain. So at last they rolled out their beds and went to sleep beside God's water hole, the nester still firm in his religious faith and fixed in his geographical convictions.

The great Block Ranch, spread out in the far-reaching shadows of the towering Capitan, furnished them plenty of action. Smith and Pattullo took up their trip again, stopping at a bar, an old hangout of Billy the Kid, as they made their way back to the settlements. Inside lounged three of the toughest-looking hombres Pattullo had ever seen. To the bartender's inquiring glance his answer was economically Scotch:

"Straight whiskey."

"Sarsaparilla!" added the abstinent Erwin.

24

"What?" asked the bartender, sharply if not incredulously.

"The same," Erwin answered, nodding at the doughty Pattullo.

The season passed with Smith getting his pictures and Pattullo soaking up ideas, color, and material for his stories. That fall they headed east again. Pattullo visited his people in Montreal, while Smith went on to Boston and took spacious quarters for them both on the top floor of Trinity Court. There with a workroom and a skylight favorable for Erwin's modeling, a desk at which Pattullo could write, and a curtain that cut their "studio" off from their bedroom, they settled down to work. Busy days passed. Erwin sketched and modeled, and the imaginative Pattullo, with vigor, confidence, and enthusiasm to spare, pounded out the stories—illustrated at first with Smith's pictures—that catapulted him to the top with the *Saturday Evening Post.*

Work aside, Boston was then not a bad place to be. There were social occasions when Erwin's sister Albert, from nearby Smith College, and other young ladies were their guests for dinner. Life was really full, though the young men's purses were sorely tried by levies for the opera, Caruso and Constantino in *La Boheme,* and John Drew, Julia Marlowe, and others on the stage. For Smith and Pattullo the arrangement was a warm, though to some a strange, collaboration: the lively, aggressive Pattullo and the quiet, retiring Smith. There was much to talk about. Yet at times, of an evening, they just sat for hours in thought without saying a word, Erwin before his little desk and Pattullo puffing on his pipe, their spirits adventuring in the West.

On the wall hung a painting of a horse standing with one hip dropped down, characteristically at ease. Next to it, above Erwin's desk, was an autographed picture of Julia Marlowe as Katherine in *The Taming of the Shrew,* and balancing it on the right was one of a figure in white, suggestive of romance that never quite materialized. In the center a Remington calendar made note of the passing days, while just beneath that the brooding face of an Indian—one of Smith's finest models, later lost during a collaboration with Gutzon Borglum—looked down from its base on the roll-top desk. In the corner just beyond, Erwin's arsenal, consisting of eight rifles, was stacked helter-skelter. In this setting Smith and Pattullo lived and dreamed and worked together for many months.

The setting was suggestive only. Far away the eternal winds blowing through the cracks of cow camps in the open country were siren songs for them. In 1909 they rolled their beds and sacked their saddles and headed back for the range. They took the train to the border, got off at Hereford, in southern Arizona, and joined the outfits that swept the scattered cattle into great herds on Bill Greene's fabulous holdings. They worked through his extensive RO range, on the Arizona side, and then crossed the border into Sonora to ride long and far with Frank Moson, Greene's general manager, through the roundups on the Turkey Tracks and the OR. Cowboy life there, where space, freedom, refuge, and adventure had brought the best from Texas and elsewhere who were born to chafe under rule and convention but never tire of the saddle—life there was a cowboy's dream. There Erwin capped off his work with the best photographic material he had ever found, while Pattullo wrote back that he had "secured more material here for stories than in all our other jauntings combined."[9]

In 1910 the two were back in Texas, making their way to the SMS, the Spurs, the Pitchforks, and again to the Matador country. For three years they consistently worked to swab the sources of fact and fiction dry in their eager quest for material. With enterprise and imaginative genius they covered a vast country, tapping the richest sources of information among the most prominent pioneers. They spent a week with the stimulating Charles Goodnight, veteran of the range and trail. They visited long with "Paint" Campbell, colorful founder of the Matadors. They spent days with the first hardy adventurer to settle on the Blanco, Hank Smith, visited profitably with the capable Frank Hastings, manager of the SMS, and made up an album while visiting with the cultivated Charles Jones, of the Spurs.

They listened to old Frank Patton as he, fortified with a handy jug, fiddled before the fireplace on the Blocks. They mingled with those superb frontier officers, Jeff Milton and Emilio Kosterlitzky, in Arizona and Sonora, and they rode the border ranges with the seasoned outfits that expansive Bill Greene had brought together with the fabulous copper of Cananea.

They ranged far and well and then went back to Boston to turn adventure to account. With other editors scrambling for the scripts that George Horace Lorimer did not take for the *Post,* Pattullo, bountifully productive, was going like a tall grass fire after a summer's drought. But the artistic road that Smith had taken was still completely unremunerative. In 1911 he came back to Bonham to work in a studio and a dark room in the attic of the barn, back of the family house. Pattullo came to Bonham too, to rent a place, buy a horse, and with five publishers pressing him for a book, to settle on the ambitious program of writing the great American novel.

In time all this artistic and literary activity wore the nerves of Erwin's practical step-father decidedly thin. Domestic troubles came. In dissension Erwin's mother sided with the children. Separation followed. Soon a division of property had to be made. Although Erwin had involved the Fannin County lands inherited from his father with mortgages, he was totally oblivious to the effects of heavy debt. He began an expensive program of improvement, stocked the place with fine cattle, and converted it into a ranch. By 1912 he was optimistically involved. Sculpture could still wait.

Yet life with cattle and horses on the lovely grasslands along Red River was mighty close to the apogee of his hopes. With dreaming youth, technique, art, and even life itself can seem to wait. But with the cumulative force of nature's seasons, time and debt do not.

[9] George Pattullo to Erwin E. Smith, October 18, 1909. This period is reconstructed from the Pattullo-Smith correspondence through the courtesy of Mrs. L. M. Pettis, Smith's sister, at Washington, D.C., and through interviews, George Pattullo to J. E. H., May 18, 1952, and Mrs. Pettis to J. E. H., May 21, 1952.

Thus Erwin Smith labored with the soil in the production of meat as the years loped on. Interest compounded with his problems, yet he never seemed to comprehend the nature of the major one he faced. The lush land responded to rain and sun with the rhythm of the seasons, and each day, as to all the men of grass, brought its own pressing and vital problem. There was always ample time for the fruition of his dreams. But the brooding face of his silent companion, the Indian on the shelf, and the deeply eroded lines in old Bomar's countenance belied the artist's perennially optimistic view, while time and posthole diggers stiffened the sensitive hands that had turned the clay to living account.

Still the years were full of plans. Smith had long been in touch with Emerson Hough, in embattled defense of the real cowboy, and Hough responded with reminiscences of the Blocks and Lincoln County, New Mexico, where he had worked in the eighties, "at a time when most of us were of the belief that we were just human beings," he observed. "But I can see now," he concluded with humor, "that we were exceedingly wild and picturesque."[10]

For a while Erwin cherished plans of an extensive trip to record the life of the Gauchos, the cowboys of the Argentine. When the Mexican Revolution broke, he and Pattullo made immediate plans to enter Mexico and cover the bloodshed and progress there. Yet men cannot casually lope off and leave a ranch, which Joe Evans once defined as a place with a herd of cattle completely surrounded with cowboys and mortgages.

During this period the Eastman Kodak Company, impressed by Smith's photographic art, prepared and sent a traveling exhibit of it about the country. His early ambition for a handsome book of his prints waxed and waned for forty years. He had thought the idea out as early as 1908. In May, 1910, he discussed the matter with Pattullo, and by October of that year the persuasive writer had convinced the hard-crusted Ferris Greenslet, of Houghton Mifflin, that such a book was full of merit and not devoid of dollars.[11] Yet then, as now, the reproductive processes were expensive, and publishers were hard to sell. At last the album or folio was fairly projected, and Erwin, with Pattullo's sound financial coaching, decided on a counter offer from Houghton Mifflin by which, instead of the usual royalties, he would share in the profits from the volume. But the variegated problems of the active cowman are constantly and vitally pressing, and in his grim struggle for life, cultivated living usually has to wait. The opportunity passed; the dream alone remained.

Like most cowmen, Erwin Smith wanted more extensive holdings. He therefore expanded the venture called Bermuda Ranch, multiplying his problems. Tragically, in 1916, his step-father died of pneumonia while on the verge of a family reconciliation. Had this come about, it is quite possible that White, as a sound businessman, would have relieved Erwin of the confusing problems successful operation of property entails, and

[10] Emerson Hough to Erwin E. Smith, December 21, 1908, Mrs. L. M. Pettis collection.

[11] The original plan for this book is detailed in several letters, George Pattullo to Tex Smith, May 7 and October 13, 1910, and February 18 and 23, 1911, Mrs. L. M. Pettis collection.

thus allowed him to return to his sculpture. Instead, the following year his mother sold the large frame house in Bonham and threw her community property into his ventures. It was a mean period for the fortunes of the range. Like a weak cow floundering deeper into the Canadian quicksands, Erwin completely exhausted his resources. Deflation took him. Foreclosure followed.

Beyond the toils of the courts of bankruptcy were his two great intangible assets: his love and intimate knowledge of the West and his capacity to sit and dream. There was still time, Erwin reasoned, to disabuse the public of its juvenile notions of the cowboy—impressions cultivated by specious literature and spurious arts of stage, brush, and screen—by showing him as he really was, a hired hand on horseback, "a man with work to do." [12]

Erwin knew of my own attempts at history before we met, and soon thereafter proposed that I write the text for a book of pictures that would truly suggest the life we had both lived to love. With his passion for quality, he insisted it should be printed in the finest form. The costs seemed to make the idea prohibitive. Meanwhile, throughout the years, he dilatorily responded to the pleas of his closest friends for choice illustrative morsels from his great collection, but made little attempt to commercialize their use in spite of their obvious value and his equally obvious need.

At one time he issued a folder offering fine prints of his "Pictures of the West," and ran an advertisement with illustration in *Scribner's,* in January, 1921. The response was startling. Among his letters were enthusiastic orders from throughout the world—from Barclay's Bank in England, a titled gentleman in London, a mounted policeman in the Yukon Territory, two Indians in Bombay, a lady in Costa Rica, an army captain in Panama, a native of Mexico City, and others from Nicaragua, Bermuda, Ecuador, China, and even California. He did not fill an order. To his mother's impatient inquiry he simply said that he "wanted to see if people were interested." It was good to know that they were, but filling orders was bothersome business.

After 1932 he lived on a small place in Fannin County owned by Mary Alice Pettis, his half-sister, where he raised a few cattle, pottered around with his pictures, and quietly dreamed of that sere world to the west, where, irrespective of weather and hours, other lean men were riding through the arid wind and sun in pursuit of honest work. Here he modestly lived with his mother, to whom he "owed his talent," and for whom, despite his seemingly irresponsible nature, he felt deep concern.

"I would like her last years to be her best years," he wrote to Mary Alice. "She has a genuine love of the country and wild life as much as I. Her intense interest in things and people constitutes a rare quality in one of her age. And she never fails to charm the few visitors I have here."

[12] As outlined to his friends Pattullo, Steger, Wharton, this writer, and others when they first met. See especially Steger, in *Holland's Magazine,* June, 1909, p. 26.

There they lived until she died, February 5, 1947, after having sacrificed marriage, home, fortune, and the better part of life in fond and hopeful nurture of the talent of her son. On September 4, seven months later, he followed from the tortures of malignancy, and was buried in Honey Grove. With precocious purpose, as Steger had written nearly forty years before, "all his life he had one central idea — to make himself a full authority on the West and to record it truly in pictures and in statuary." Careful plans were recurrently laid, but not a cast was ever done. When man's potential is actually measured against life's frustrations, he inclines to wonder if there is ever "ample time."

Despite my repeated emphasis of the historical value of cataloguing his immense collection, and efforts to get it done, Smith never found time, though his recollection of time and place, and the horses and men involved, was nothing short of remarkable. When approached on the subject, Smith would agree as to the need; then, like as not, with that faraway look in his eyes, he'd say: "There are two great collections of Western pictures that we've got to find and save — that by L. A. Huffman, of Montana, and the other by M. C. Ragsdale, of San Angelo." As for his own, well, we would get around to it in time.

Two years after his death, his talented sister, Mrs. L. M. Pettis, of Washington, D.C., took more than eighteen hundred of his cherished plates and films out of storage and gave them to the Library of Congress. There, for more than a year, Ona Lee McKeen, with the help of George Pattullo and others, worked in an attempt to catalogue them. But the primary source is gone. The job will never be done.

In 1936, at my insistence, Erwin Smith prepared one hundred of his best prints for display during the Texas Centennial, which were eventually placed in the Texas Memorial Museum at Austin. When they fell under the appraising eye of Frank Wardlaw, director of the University of Texas Press, he at once conceived the idea of converting them into a book which would be a true picture of the Texas range. At the suggestion of historian Walter P. Webb, Wardlaw pried me loose from work with cattle and horses — from the problems of life as derived from grass — long enough to write the text.

Thus Erwin E. Smith's long dream of an appropriate book of his prints is at last fulfilled. To quote my past master of history, Dr. E. C. Barker, of the University of Texas, as he came to the end of his monumental work on Stephen F. Austin, "There is a certain poetic completeness in this. But the prosaic mind rebels." It seems a tragic, perverse fate that a sensitive, devoted, talented man must be dead for years before his life's ambition is realized. Yet it may indicate that ample and indefinite time really favors those who dream unselfishly and well.

JH Ranch   J. EVETTS HALEY
June 25, 1952

Plates

CHUCK WAGON ON THE MOVE

The wagon, home of the cowboy on the larger
outfits, is pulled out on the spring roundup with
bedrolls stacked to the wagon bows and four
slick mules in their collars. The boss leads the
way to pick the camp.

PITCHING CAMP

This outfit, with variegated team, is pitching camp below a shinnery-covered sand dune. All hands turn in to help the lordly cook unhook his team and roll off the beds.

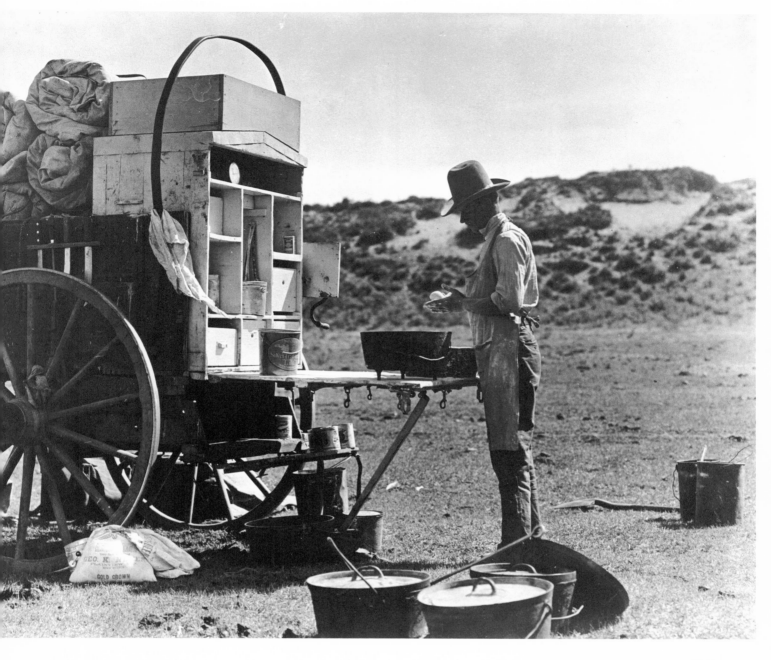

SOUR DOUGH FOR DINNER

After mixing his batch of biscuits in the dishpan on the lowered chuck-box lid, the cook deftly rolls them out between his hands, turns them in melted grease, and bakes them in a skillet and lid —a Dutch oven.

"COME AND GIT IT!"

The cook's long-awaited roar of "Chuck!" or "Come and git it!" starts a stampede among the men, in the saddle since four in the morning. All hands are willing.

CHUCK

A Mexican-border outfit "gits it." Cow-camp
meals are quiet, businesslike affairs. Conversa-
tion is lacking. Cowboys eat, pitch their tin plates
and cups into the cook's roundup—his dishpan
or a wash tub that amply serves the purpose—
mount, and head back to the herd.

TWO RANGE OUTFITS CAMP TOGETHER

In this vast range where shinnery has given way to greasewood, sand, and space, dinner is over and the dishwater boils on the pot rack while the cowboys are catching fresh horses before going back to the herd.

CLEANING UP

With dishpan poised on his sour-dough keg, and the chuck-box lid as his draining board, the cook washes the dishes while the horse wrangler dries them with a dingy cloth and rattles them into the lower drawer.

THE DAY HERDER COMES IN TO EAT

While the crew is eating, the herd must be held. Then the day herders come in to eat. This hungry rider has set his coffee on the chuck-box lid and taken his beef and bread in hand. His horse, with dragging reins, patiently awaits his return.

LONG SHADOWS AND EARLY SUPPER

With fresh beef quarters hung out to cool, some beds spread for early sleep, and the first guard eating supper, work goes on after night comes in the cow country. The day herd, in perfect formation on the hill beyond, will be held in close herd through the night.

PICKING A SIDE OF BARBECUED RIBS

With the cook's indulgence, the Shoe Bar boys of the Red River country use pocket knives and fingers to pick a side of ribs as an appetizer before supper. The cook is busy at his box beneath the canvas fly.

BREAKFAST AT 4 A.M. ON THE JA

In the luminous glow of a mesquite fire this pioneer outfit of the Plains fortifies all hands with fried steak and coffee for the rough riding ahead.

SHOE BARS CATCHING HORSES

Horses were trained to stand in corrals formed by stretched catch-ropes. Here the boss ropes out each man's mount as the rider calls his preference: "Gimme Old Gotch," "Widder-Maker," "Shorty," ...

A BORDER BOSS TELLING OFF HIS RIDERS

The crew has pulled out on the drive together. Miles away from the wagon, the boss draws rein and "tells off" his riders, giving each his place on the drive.

THE DRIVE

The act of rounding-up is called the drive. After being told off, the widely scattered men, swinging at a high lope in a gigantic circle, begin throwing the drive together.

ON THE ROUNDUP GROUND

As the riders converge, the drive is thrown upon the roundup ground. Here a herd, well-spaced for proper working, is held at the base of the Texas Plains.

DAY HERD ON THE SPURS

Three cowpunchers get together for a little "augurin'" as they hold a quiet day herd on the Spurs. The cattle are held for further work —cutting, shaping-up, and branding.

PICKING HIS MATADOR COW

This "stray man," representing the neighboring
Matador outfit, is prowling through the roundup
to pick his strays.

CUTTING HER OUT

With his real cutting horse in action, and his wild, red-eyed cow with the Matador *V* upon her ribs headed for the tall uncut, the stray man brings her out, and under control.

WORKING THE ROUNDUP

The fine art of cutting cattle without unduly disturbing the herd is known as working the round-up. It calls for intimate knowledge of animal nature on the part of both men and horses.

TURNING ON A DIME

To outmaneuver a snaky cow requires the utmost coordination of mount and man. It takes natural aptitude, zest for the work, action, intelligence, and long years of training to make a horse like this.

HOLDING AN LS HERD

After the work is done, the herd is usually held until the cows and scattered calves are mated up. This tired cowboy on the Canadian River, with hatband askew, slumps on his saddle horn in the outfit's sleepiest job.

HEELING

The old outfits branded on the open range. Cowboys held the herd while two ropers dragged out the calves. It was easy to tail them over when they were heeled.

THE CALF-ROPER

The roper heels a calf and drags him to the fire.
He is held by the flankers while the brander
applies the hot iron and another puncher wields
the knife in cutting and marking.

DRAGGING HIM TO THE FIRE

Sometimes the roper catches the calf around the neck and drags him to the branding fire. Sets of flankers go down the line to meet the pitching, "bellering" calves and "lay them on the sod."

FLANKING A BIG ONE

Here a real flanker, with right hand thrown across the animal's back into the off-flank and left hand on the rope, catches the animal on the jump and suns his heels.

HOT IRON AND SHARP KNIFE

As the flanker lays the calf on the ground, his partner quickly grabs the animal's heels to keep him from kicking loose. Hot iron and sharp knife are already on the way.

COORDINATION WITH COWS

The roper swings his horse around and, as the flanker slips off the loop, rides into the herd after another calf. Here is a combination of skill and art—the prettiest work on any range.

ANXIETY OF MOTHER COWS

With many anxious eyes upon him inquiring, "Could that be my precious boy?" this big fellow is dragged to the fire by a real horse, leaning nobly to his work. Flankers fall into position on either side of the rope.

STRUNG OUT

When calves got too big to handle by hand, they were dragged from the roundup by the neck, heeled by a second roper, strung out between the two, and tailed down.

GA'NT HORSE IN A BIG COUNTRY

This stocky cowboy on a drawn horse is riding a big Canadian River range. The cattle that are his special care cover the valley beyond.

ROLLING HIS OWN ON DAY HERD

This border hand, on a better mount, stops in a
gentle breeze to roll a cigarette while herding his
old-time cattle.

COUNTING THEM OUT

Before a herd was turned loose it was common practice to count the cattle out by squeezing them down to narrow file between the riders.

TALLYING FOR THE TRAIL

Here, in closer detail, is a herd being forced between the counters in the background. The farthest rider, with raised hand, is making his count by "putting a finger on them" as they pass.

HERD FORMATION

This fine view of a herd in formation shows how millions of cattle moved off the pioneer ranges upon the Texas Trail. They grazed as they walked, but every step for grass pointed in the right direction.

MATADORS ON THE TRAIL

These narrow parallel paths, cut through the sod by thousands of flinty hoofs, constituted the cattle trails. The weaker cattle that dropped behind were the "drags."

IN THE DUST OF THE DRAGS

In contrast with the preceding picture, work with the drags was usually like this. While the hands in the lead, the pointers, are facing a bright new world, those with the drags are spitting mud and dreaming of a drink at the first bar.

THEN BARBED WIRE PLAYED HELL WITH TEXAS

Barbed wire ended the open range and revolu-
tionized the business. It came into its own in the
early eighties on the Plains of Texas. Here are
the Spurs, ignominiously caught in a wire gate.

69

SADDLE HORSES

The old Gaucho saying that "a man without a horse is a man without legs" held true in Texas. Hard and long riding in a big country required lots of horseflesh. Here it is.

LS HAND STAKING HIS NIGHT HORSE

"A man on foot was no man at all." And so the night herders staked their saddled mounts in easy distance of the wagon to be quickly at hand in case of stampede.

SHOE BAR WRANGLER RIDES A MULE

Sure-footed mules had their advantages in a rough country. This Panhandle puncher in the Red River breaks finds a gray mule to his liking. Horses may be as reckless as riders, but a mule never commits suicide.

DAY-HERDING THE REMUDA

From a vantage point on the cap rock, the wrangler watches over his grazing horses until it is time to throw them together near the wagon for the next change of mounts.

LITTLE JOE THE WRANGLER

Many tousled boys in dilapidated hats and bro-
gans, proudly sitting in old hulls above tattered
sugans for saddle blankets, got their first taste of
range life as wranglers, like "Little Joe" in the
cowboy ballad.

SMEARING HIS LOOP ON A WILD ONE

This cowpuncher, waiting his change of mount alongside the remuda, helps out the roper on the ground by smearing his loop on a wild one.

MATADOR REMUDA GOES BACK TO GRASS

After fresh mounts are caught from the rope corral, the wrangler takes the remuda back to grass, where it will be loose-herded until needed again. His partner, the "nighthawk," will take over the job beneath the stars.

TYING UP A FOOT TO SADDLE A BRONC

The first step in breaking a bronc takes place in the corral. An absolutely unruly horse can be handled by one man by tying up a foot. This alert bronc is about to be ridden his "first saddle."

A-SETTIN' IN HIS TREE

Then out in the free and wide-open world the fun begins when this unwilling bronc "swallers his head and chins the moon." The rider is "screwed down and really settin' deep in his tree."

SUNNIN' HIS SIDES

If he is never successfully broken or gentled, the bronc may find his way to the rodeo grounds. In the most vicious pitching, some horses jump high and wide and twist themselves out of the vertical, "sunnin' their sides," to test the nerviest men.

A-RARIN' TO GO

Other outlaw horses attempt to loosen their riders by rearing up and threatening to fall back. Sometimes they do go over, fatally injuring the rider. In this picture the cowboy wonders if it isn't time to leave Cheyenne.

A-LEAVIN' CHEYENNE

"So long, ladies, my horses won't stand,
 Good-bye, Old Paint, I'm a-leavin' Cheyenne."

COMING BACK DOWN THE CATTLE TRAIL

After the herds were shipped from the cow towns, prize remudas were trailed back with the wagons. Here is how they looked, strung out on the cattle trail, headed home to Texas.

PACKING THEIR BED

In the old days cowboys packed their beds across
the backs of gentle horses. A man on either side
drew the hitches tight.

LEAVING FOR THE WORK

With a coffee pot and frying pan tied on top for camping along the way, these two hands start for the roundup—the general work.

DROPPING OFF THE CAP ROCK

News of the general work reached every camp.
These men, with their personal mounts and
packed beds, are dropping off the cap rock of
the Staked Plains to join the outfits in the breaks.

CLEAR-FOOTED HORSES FOR ROUGH COUNTRY

In zestful, clear-footed stride the combined mounts of two cowpunchers swing across the breaks, headed for the general work.

COMING INTO CAMP

These two hands, with jointly packed beds, are coming into camp while their horses, with alert ears, are sizing up the place.

SHOOTIN' CRAPS

The tenderfoot, marked by rolled sleeves and the pitch of his hat, helps three seasoned hands turn a bedroll to profitable use while waiting for supper.

CLOG DANCE IN A COW CAMP

With the fiddler seated on his bedroll and a helper beating time, a clog dancer amuses the outfit, even to the cook, whose right hand aimlessly wades around in the sour dough.

MUMBLE-PEG

Diversions were few and simple. These cowboys pass the time at mumble-peg as their horses hunt a bite of grass or stand dozing in the sun, tied to their dragging bridle reins.

HUNTING SEASON AT HAND

When the fall grass put the tallow on the pronghorn's ribs, hunting season was at hand for these Matador cowboys, living in a dugout adorned with a horseshoe, coyote hide, elk horn, and a dirty towel.

HITCHING POSTS AT OLD TASCOSA

These dry Canadian River cowboys are in a hurry to get to the hitching posts at Old Tascosa, principal oasis of diversion for a vast cow country.

SETTLING THE DUST

Out of the sun, they lose no time in propping
their booted and spurred feet upon the rail and
settling the dust of Old Tascosa.

COMING INTO TOWN

Far away on the alkali flats of the Border, other thirsty hands come fogging in out of the arid space, fervidly bent on a similar mission.

CATCHING A MATADOR OUTLAW

Back on the range, work goes on. In rough or brushy country, cattle, irrespective of breed, often "outlaw," or go completely wild. Sometimes it is necessary to gather them at the end of a rope.

HOBBLING AN OUTLAW STEER

This outlaw has been roped, thrown, and hobbled so that he cannot run away. One man slips the rope from his horns as another keeps him flat by a tail hold through his flank, preparatory to turning him loose.

PICKING UP HIS HEELS

This big mottled-faced steer has been caught by
two ropers who hold him while another swings
a loop to pick up his heels and stretch him out.

TURNING AN OUTLAW LOOSE

With plenty of hands sitting round to hold this wild steer, the men on the ground are slipping off the ropes to turn him loose.

BRINGING THE HERD TO THE WILD ONE

When it is impossible to handle an outlaw alone,
he is roped and tied and a gentle bunch brought
to him. Even then he is sometimes slow to move.

TURNING HIM INTO THE GENTLE BUNCH

At last, with ropes thrown off, he gets up from the ground. With his wild and reckless spirit somewhat subdued and his freedom gone, he is trailed off with the herd and shipped to the packing plant.

FIGHTING STOCK

Whether in picket corrals or out on the range, this rough, free life still produces its fighting stock. This snuffy cow, even while stretched between two ropes, scatters all hands, who find her hard to tail down.

101

TAKING CARE OF COWS

For all its colorful action, the first work of cowboys is taking care of cows. No set routine can
meet the caprices of nature and her creatures.
These LS hands are pulling a cow from where
she has fallen beneath a large boulder.

RANGE BRANDING

Calves that were missed by the general roundup were sometimes roped, tied down, and branded on the range with a hot ring held between two short sticks.

ODD JOBS IN CAMP

Cowboys used their spare time making repairs to their saddles and other rigging, while the intellectually inclined sought culture from a paper-pulp in the shade of the wagon. These two are making a mohair cinch.

A PET HORSE GETS HIS BISCUIT

Horses, the sweethearts of the range world, were the chief competitors of the lonely girls whom cowboys had left behind in the settlements. Jake Raines, veteran of the Spurs, fed his mount on sour dough.

A RANGE MANAGER'S RIG

When age, judgment, and character turned the cowboy into a seasoned range manager, he sometimes substituted a buggy and a spanking team for his horse and saddle.

MATADOR OUTFIT IN THE EIGHTIES

This grizzled Matador outfit worked on the last of the British-owned ranges in Texas. The chuck wagon, except for its more barren aspects, closely resembles those of today.

BREEDS CHANGE BUT THE RANGE STAYS

Except for an occasional Mexican herd, such cattle as these are not seen in Texas today. Breeds come and go, but an implacable nature has decreed that land like this shall be kept for cowboys.

THE SYMBOL OF TEXAS

Wiry, free, and full of fight, the longhorn steer
is as symbolical of Texas as the Lone Star. "Other
lands were bred and born; Texas grew from hide
and horn."

THE NESTER AT THE WATER HOLE

Wherever the rain, coupled with the eager nature and ingenuity of the Western settler, was even remotely ample, the land was taken by the nester —the man with the plow, the two-horse team, the towheaded kids, and the hounds.

SUN AND SHADE

But where rain is almost nonexistent, where the blazing light of day is but rarely broken by the shade of stunted trees battling for life, the Texas cowboy is still at home. He lives in the sun with little time for shade.

STILL IN THE SUN

"Where the coyotes howl and the wind blows free ...
They buried him there on the lone prairie-e."